Let's Sightplay!
by Kathleen Massoud

Book 1
EARLY ELEMENTARY LEVEL

**Creative Solo Exercises to
Develop Sightplaying at the Piano**

CONTENTS

This book is lovingly dedicated to my husband (and best friend), Steven.

A Note to the Teacher

Developing Sightplaying Skills

Sightplaying is a valuable skill which can be developed at the earliest stages of piano study. Proficiency in sightplaying will result from instilling the good habits of thinking ahead, keeping a steady beat, using correct fingerings, and recognizing intervals and other patterns.

Teachers will appreciate improved weekly lessons as students learn to pay closer attention to what is written on the page. When sightplaying is an integral part of weekly lessons, it becomes regarded as an attainable skill instead of one reserved just for "gifted" students.

Let's Sightplay! includes a variety of short exercises designed to drill the important elements of sightplaying, but always within a musical context.

How to Use This Book

Sightplaying refers to the first attempts at playing music that has never been tried before. It is not limited to just the first reading. Students should be encouraged to play exercises several times if they cannot accurately digest all the musical information on the first try.

The exercises in this book have been grouped into fourteen "Lessons," each with four different exercises. During the piano lesson, teachers may choose to hear any of the four exercises, with the remainder to be tried at home in order to save lesson time. It is important for students to understand that after each exercise can be played completely accurately, it is not to be practiced further. (Students may record in the book how many tries it takes to reach an accurate performance level.)

Motivating Students

Sightplaying should always emphasize accuracy as well as not stopping despite difficulties. One effective method to encourage students to value accuracy is by allowing them to earn points for accurate sightplaying.

In this book, points may be awarded according to how many tries it takes to play an exercise accurately. If the student is successful on the first try, that is worth 30 points; the second try, 20 points; and the third try, 10 points. (The teacher may use discretion to make these goals flexible and attainable by even the slowest student's best efforts.) Test exercises may include either new exercises or those assigned the previous week. If two exercises are tested, the student, at best, could earn up to 60 points. for every 100 points earned, it is suggested that the student may receive an incentive, such as a "composer stamp" or a special sticker.

Let's Sightplay! aims to make sightplaying into a challenging game, which in turn will make students respond with more concentration and effort.

A Note to the Student

Welcome to the world of sightplaying!

Here is a checklist you can use to help you sightplay better:

1. What does the time signature tell you in the music? **Always count one measure aloud before starting.** (It's best to keep counting aloud as you play!)

2. What is the **first note** and **finger number** for the right hand?
    What is the **first note** and **finger number** for the left hand?

3. Can you follow the melody from one hand to the other? **Always look ahead!**

4. Do you see any tricky rhythms? Be on the lookout for ties and rests!

5. Are there places where both hands play together?

6. Are there places where one hand plays two notes together? **Is the interval a 2nd (step) or a 3rd (skip)?**

7. Do you see any note patterns that happen more than once? **It helps to find any measures that look alike.**

8. Do you see any dynamic marks (loud and soft)? Dynamic marks will make the music sound more interesting!

In each lesson in this book, you will find some **"Sightplaying Hints"** which you should read **before** sightplaying the exercises. These hints will help you notice things in the music so that you will sightplay more accurately.

FJH1114

Lesson One

1 Dialogue

A Joyful Song

SIGHTPLAYING HINT:
Count one measure aloud before playing.

mf

2 Sightplaying Chimes

Extra Credit: Metronome clicks
♩ = ☐ on every half note.

♩ = ☐

*depress pedal

lift pedal

3 Sightplaying Chimes

Extra Credit: Metronome clicks
♩ = ☐ on every half note.

♩ = ☐

depress pedal

lift pedal

*All the Sightplaying Chimes in this book are to be played with the right foot (damper) pedal down.

4A THEME

Dance With Me

SIGHTPLAYING HINT:
What does the time signature mean in this piece?

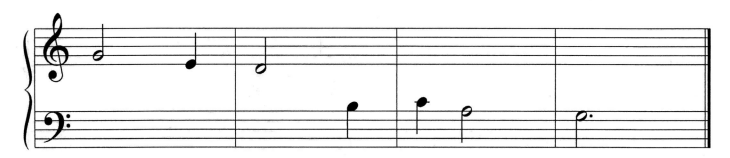

4B VARIATION

Come Fly With Me

SIGHTPLAYING HINT:
The dotted lines will help your eyes follow the melody. Always remember to look ahead from **left to right.** →

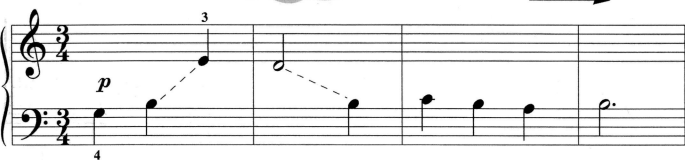

Lesson One total points* ☐

* (Teacher: see "Motivating Students," page 2.)

FJH1114

6

Lesson Two

5 Dialogue

Sneaky Footsteps

SIGHTPLAYING HINT:
Be on the lookout for (sneaky) rests!

Very softly!

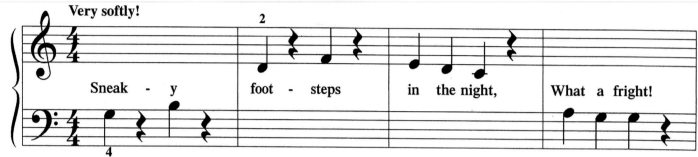

Sneak - y | foot - steps | in the night, | What a fright!

Sneak - y | foot - steps, who | can it be? | (It's me!)

6 Sightplaying Chimes

♩ = ☐

Extra Credit: Metronome clicks on every half note. ♩ = ☐

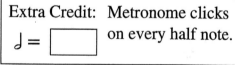

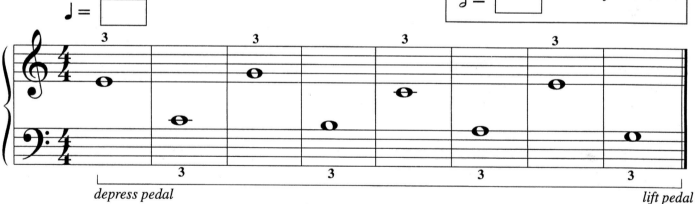

depress pedal   *lift pedal*

7 Sightplaying Chimes

♩ = ☐

Extra Credit: Metronome clicks on every half note. ♩ = ☐

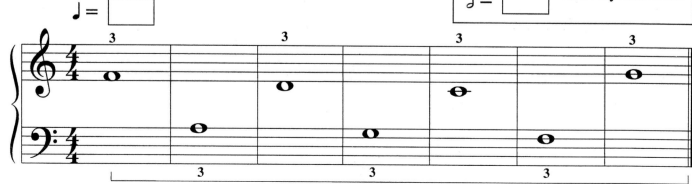

8A THEME

Wintertime Is Near

SIGHTPLAYING HINT:
Choose a comfortable tempo (not too fast!) so you will have enough time to look ahead.

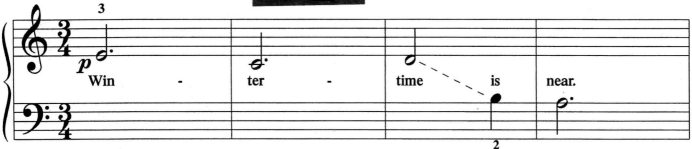

Win - ter - time is near.

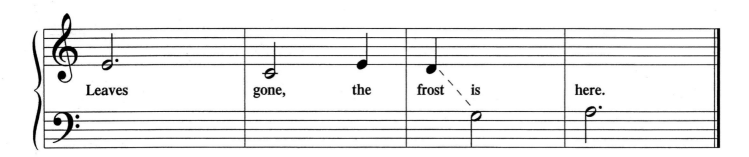

Leaves gone, the frost is here.

8B VARIATION

Snowflakes Are Falling

SIGHTPLAYING HINT:
Compare measure 3 of this Variation with measure 3 of the Theme.

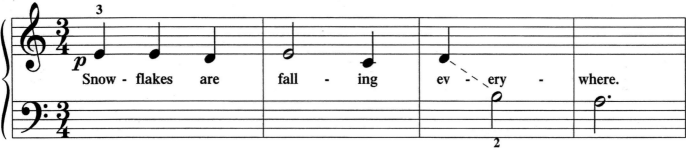

Snow - flakes are fall - ing ev - ery - where.

Beau - ti - ful snow - flakes drift through the air.

Lesson Two total points ☐

FJH1114

Lesson Three

9 Dialogue

On The Prairie

SIGHTPLAYING HINT:
Be sure to count the last two measures carefully!

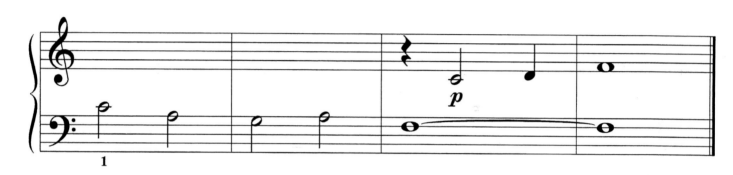

10 Sightplaying Chimes

♩ = [ ]

Extra Credit:
♩ = [ ]

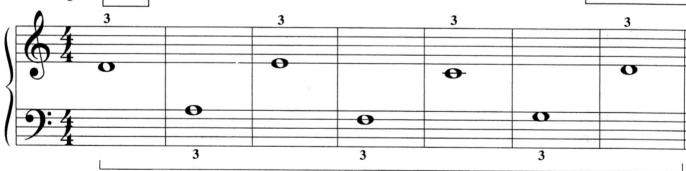

11 Sightplaying Chimes

♩ = [ ]

Extra Credit:
♩ = [ ]

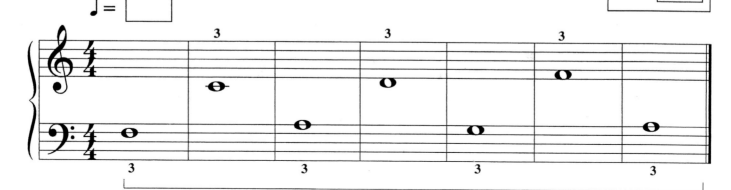

12A THEME

Sound The Trumpets!

SIGHTPLAYING HINT:
Can you find some measures that repeat?

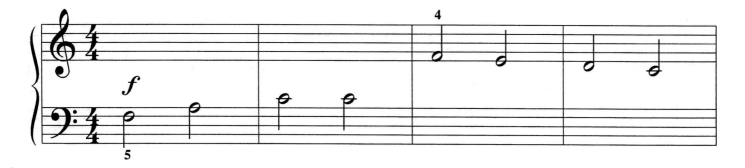

12B VARIATION

Raise The Banner!

SIGHTPLAYING HINT:
How is the first measure of "Raise the Banner" different from the first measure of "Sound the Trumpets"?

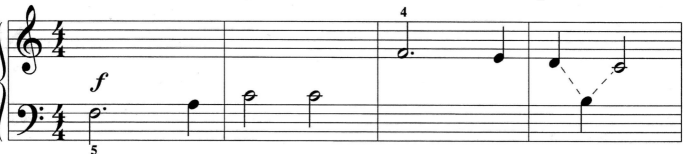

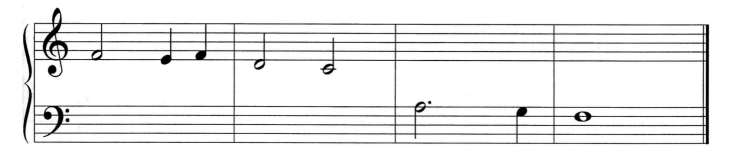

Lesson Three total points ☐

FJH1114

Lesson Four

13 Dialogue

Joy In The Morning

SIGHTPLAYING HINT:
Try playing this piece without looking down at your hands. Trust your eyes and your fingers!

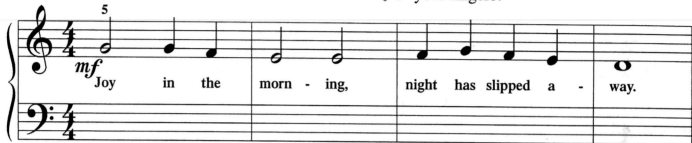

Joy   in   the   morn - ing,   night   has   slipped   a - way.

Joy   in   the   morn - ing,   it's   a   brand - new   day.

14 Sightplaying Chimes

Extra Credit:

♩ = [ ]

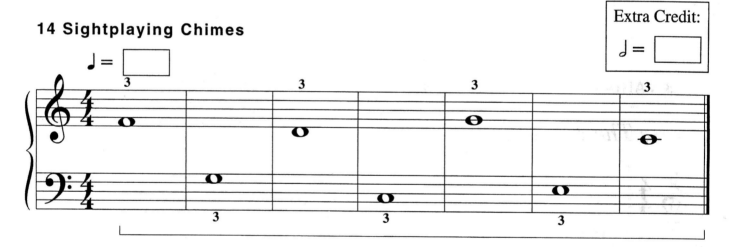

15 Echo Chimes*

Extra Credit:

♩ = [ ]

You write these echo notes!

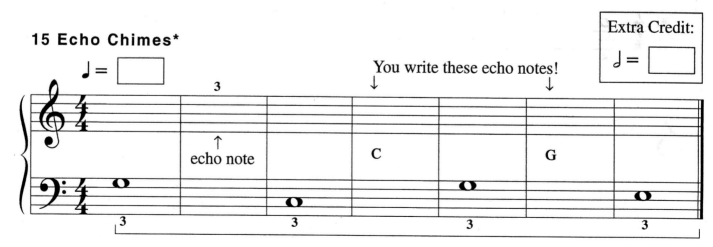

echo note   C   G

*The **echo note** has the **same note name** as the note before it.
  In the blank measures, write the missing echo notes in the treble clef before playing.

16A THEME

Flying Carpet . . .

SIGHTPLAYING HINT:
Make sure each hand starts on the correct note with the correct fingering.

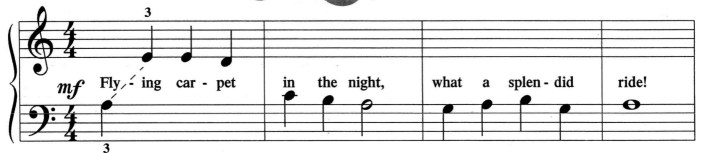

Fly - ing car - pet in the night, what a splen - did ride!

Com - fy seats and what a view! See far and wide...

16B VARIATION

. . . Over The Desert

SIGHTPLAYING HINT:
Try tapping the rhythm before sightplaying.

Lesson Four total points ☐

FJH1114

Lesson Five

17 Dialogue

Tiptoe!

Tip - toe, tip - toe, in the house, like a mouse, I'll be qui - et as can be. No one can hear me!

18 Sightplaying Chimes

Extra Credit:

19 Echo Chimes*

Extra Credit:

echo note

You write these echo notes!

*The **echo note** has the **same note name** as the note before it.
In the blank measures, write the missing echo notes in the bass clef before playing.

20A THEME

Apple Blossoms

SIGHTPLAYING HINT:
This piece has two different dynamic marks. (Read the words to find out why!)

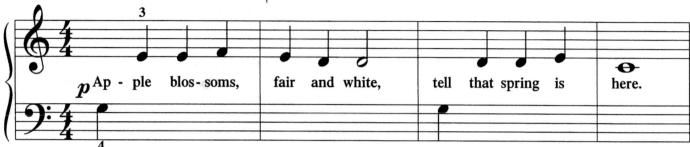

p Ap - ple blos - soms, | fair and white, | tell that spring is | here.

Bees are buzz - ing | 'round a - bout. | Care - ful, don't come | near!
mf

20B VARIATION

Tulip Time

SIGHTPLAYING HINT:
Be sure to play the notes as they appear from left to right. (There are no dotted lines to help!)

mf

Lesson Five total points ☐

14

Lesson Six

21 Dialogue

Strawberry Ice Cream

SIGHTPLAYING HINT:
Find the two places where both hands play together. Look ahead and be prepared!

Straw - ber - ry   ice   cream!   Ma - ma,   please   get   me   some

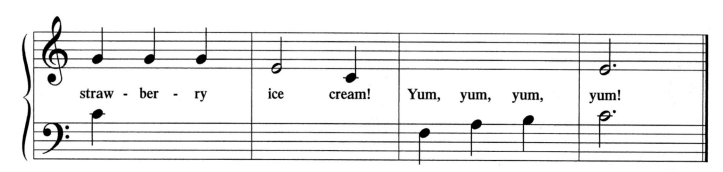

straw - ber - ry   ice   cream!   Yum,   yum,   yum,   yum!

22 Sightplaying Chimes

Extra Credit:

♩ = ▢

♩ = ▢

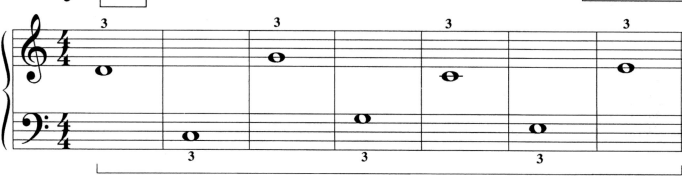

23 Echo Chimes   (Write the echo notes before playing.)

Extra Credit:

♩ = ▢

♩ = ▢

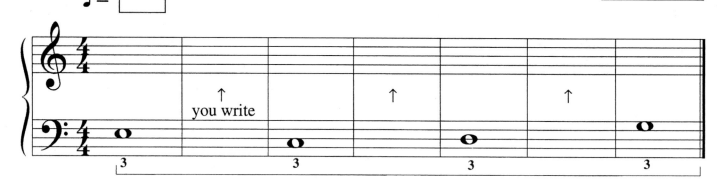

you write

FJH1114

24A THEME

Mister Ice Cream Man

SIGHTPLAYING HINT:
How many **3rds** (skips) can you find?
(Answer: ⬚)

24B VARIATION

Waltz of the Ice Cream Cones

SIGHTPLAYING HINT:
Count one measure aloud before starting
and keep **counting aloud** as you play.

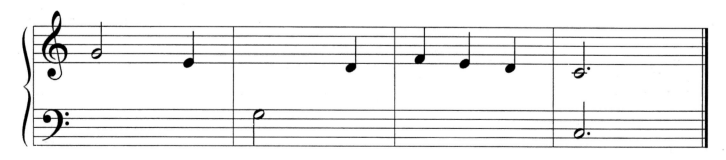

Lesson Six total points ⬚

Lesson Seven

25 Dialogue

Little Shining Star

SIGHTPLAYING HINT:
Try to play "Little Shining Star" without looking down at your hands.

Lit - tle shin - ing star, high up in the sky,

I'll make a wish on you, lit - tle shin - ing star.

26 Sightplaying Chimes

♩ = [　　]

Extra Credit:
♩ = [　　]

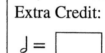

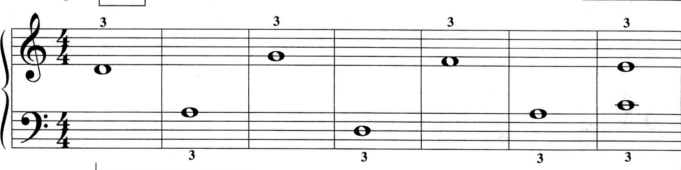

27 Echo Chimes

(Write the echo notes before playing.)

Extra Credit:
♩ = [　　]

♩ = [　　]

you write

28A THEME

Voyage Into Space

SIGHTPLAYING HINT:
When coming to the end of a line, always look ahead! What interval do you see in measure 5?

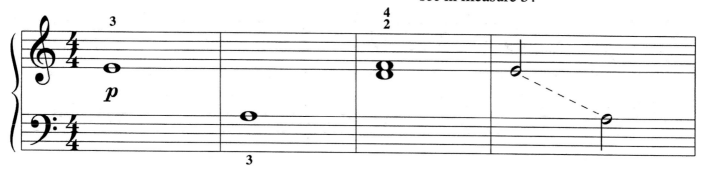

28B VARIATION

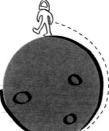

Walking On The Moon

SIGHTPLAYING HINT:
Choose a comfortable tempo, so the music will be smooth and steady!

With our space boots we can walk on the moon.

We can go ex - plor - ing and be home by noon!

Lesson Seven total points ☐

FJH1114

Lesson Eight

29 Dialogue

SIGHTPLAYING HINT:
Keep your eyes on the music, and trust
your fingers to play the intervals.

Follow the Rainbow

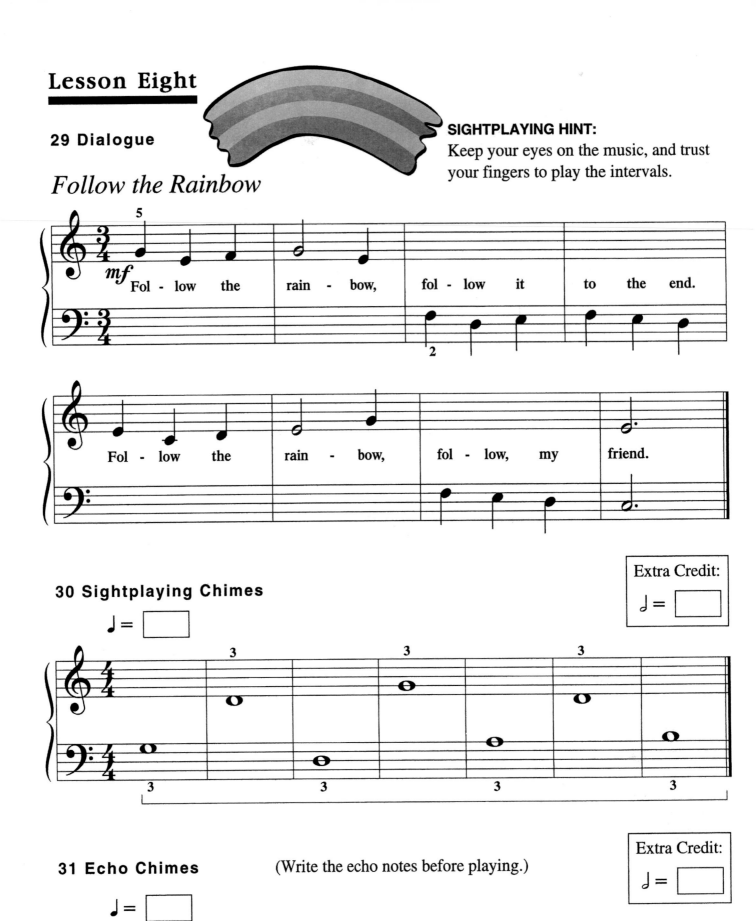

30 Sightplaying Chimes

Extra Credit:

31 Echo Chimes   (Write the echo notes before playing.)

Extra Credit:

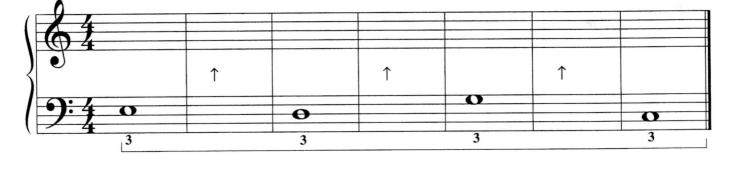

FJH1114

32A THEME

Swing Your Partner!

SIGHTPLAYING HINT:
Find any measures that look exactly alike. Music often has **note patterns** that appear more than once.

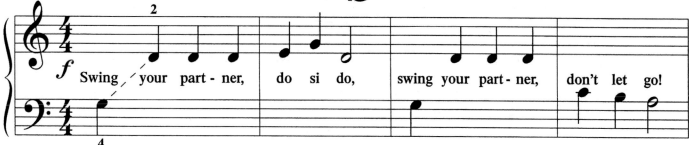

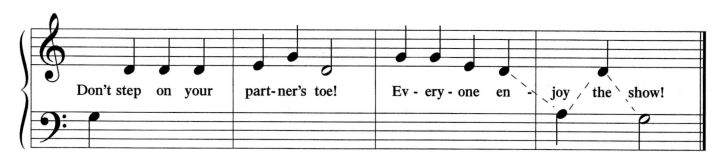

32B VARIATION

Dance To The Music!

SIGHTPLAYING HINT:
Tap the **rhythm** before playing.

Lesson Eight total points ☐

Lesson Nine

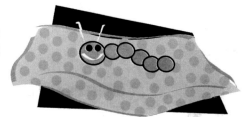

33 Dialogue

SIGHTPLAYING HINT:
Be on the lookout for repeated notes!

Caterpillar On My Bed

Cat - er - pil - lar on my bed, guess it's just a sleep - y head.

Just like me, it needs a rest. Sleep now, cat - er - pil - lar.

34 Sightplaying Chimes

Extra Credit:
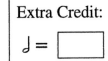

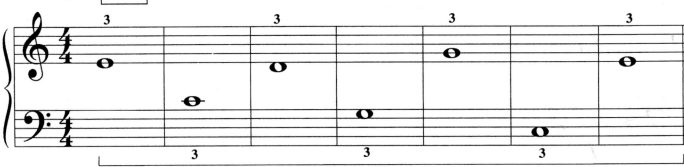

35 Echo Chimes

(Write the echo notes before playing.)

Extra Credit:

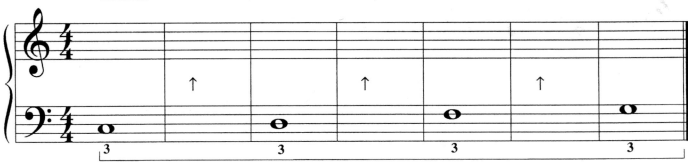

36A THEME

Sail On A Moonbeam

SIGHTPLAYING HINT:
Do you see any measures that are **exactly** the same?

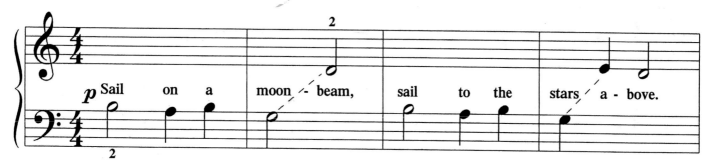

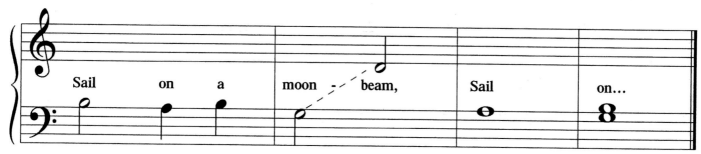

36B VARIATION

Make A Wish

SIGHTPLAYING HINT:
Notice the tied notes in the second line.

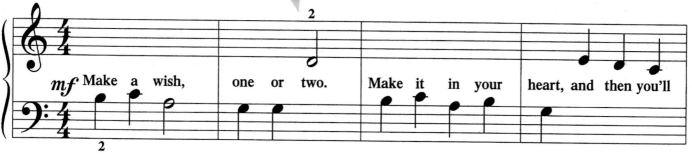

Lesson Nine total points ☐

FJH1114

Lesson Ten

37 Dialogue

Russian Song

SIGHTPLAYING HINT:
At the place where the hands play together, write the fingering you plan to use.

38 Sightplaying Chimes

39 Echo Chimes

(Write the echo notes before playing.)

40A THEME

Clock Strikes Twelve

SIGHTPLAYING HINT:
Can you find any measures where the R.H. does NOT play repeated notes?

(half rest)

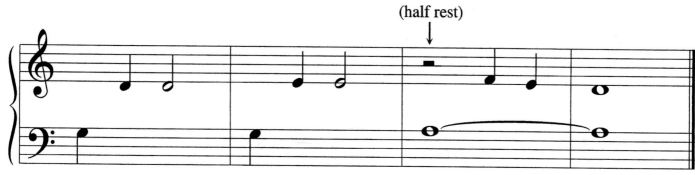

40B VARIATION

Midnight Hour

SIGHTPLAYING HINT:
Find any measures that are **exactly** alike. What interval is used the most in this piece?

Lesson Ten total points ☐

FJH1114

Lesson Eleven

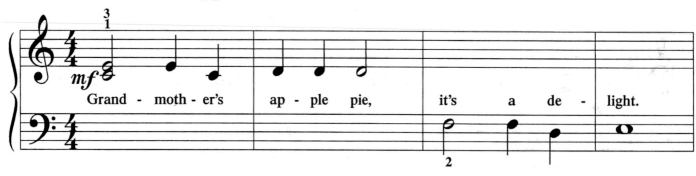

41 Dialogue

m m m m

SIGHTPLAYING HINT:
Find the intervals that are played
together. Can you name them?

Grandmother's Apple Pie

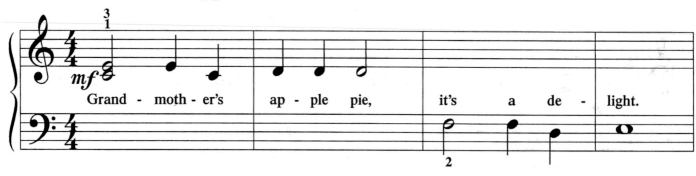

Grand - moth - er's ap - ple pie, it's a de - light.

Topped with fresh whipped cream, it tastes just right!

42 Sightplaying Chimes

Extra Credit:

♩ = ☐

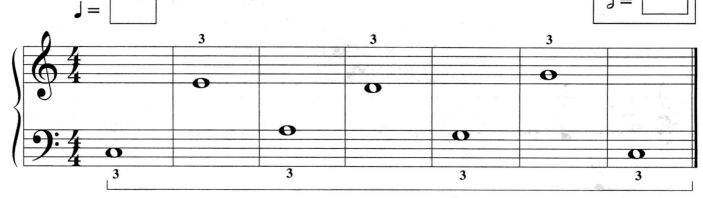

43 Echo Chimes   (Write the echo notes before playing.)

Extra Credit:

♩ = ☐

FJH1114

44A THEME

It's That Time Again . . .

SIGHTPLAYING HINT:
The notes in the last two measures are far apart. Try to play them without looking down!

44B VARIATION

. . . To Practice!

SIGHTPLAYING HINT:
How many different notes does the L.H. play in this piece?

Lesson Eleven total points ☐

FJH1114

26

Lesson Twelve

45 Dialogue

Alleluia

SIGHTPLAYING HINT:
Be ready to play **hands together** at measure 7, and try to keep a **steady beat.**

Al - le - lu - ia.

Al - le - lu - ia.

46 Sightplaying Chimes

Extra Credit:

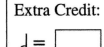

47 Echo Chimes

(Write the echo notes before playing.)

Extra Credit:

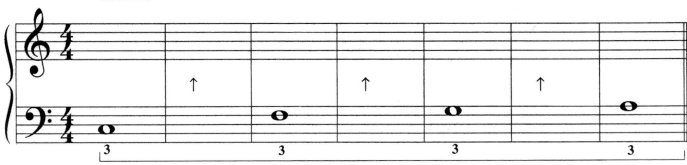

48A THEME

Dandelion Polka

SIGHTPLAYING HINT:
Make sure your eyes **follow** the **melody**
as it goes from one hand to the other.

48B VARIATION

Violet Waltz

SIGHTPLAYING HINT:
Do you see any note patterns here that
remind you of "Dandelion Polka"?

Lesson Twelve total points

Lesson Thirteen

49 Dialogue

SIGHTPLAYING HINT:
Be sure to count the **rests** carefully!

The Tired Metronome

50 Sightplaying Chimes

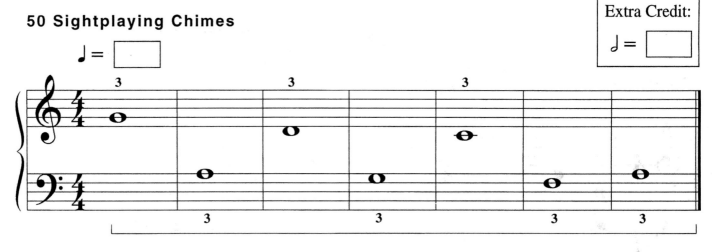

51 Echo Chimes

(Write the echo notes before playing.)

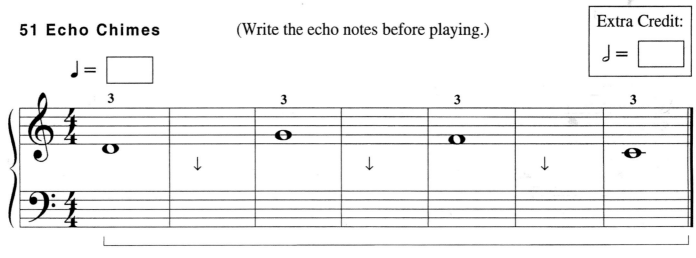

52A THEME

Far Away

SIGHTPLAYING HINT:
Be sure each hand starts on the **correct note** with the **correct fingering.** Write the L.H. fingering in the boxes.

52B VARIATION

A Distant Voice

SIGHTPLAYING HINT:
Compare the last line of "A Distant Voice" with the last line of "Far Away." How are they different?

Lesson Thirteen total points

FJH1114

Lesson Fourteen

53 Dialogue

Get Up!

SIGHTPLAYING HINT:
The circled finger number ① means there is a **hand position change.** Be prepared!

54 Sightplaying Chimes

Extra Credit:

55 Echo Chimes   (Write the echo notes before playing.)

Extra Credit:

56A THEME

Watch Your Step!

SIGHTPLAYING HINT:
On the keyboard, silently find the hand positions used in measure 1, measure 2, and measure 3. Are any the same?

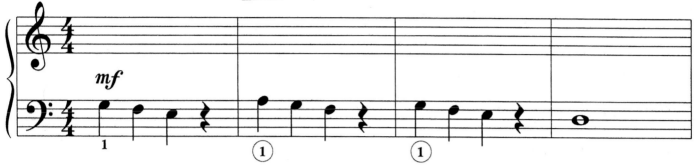

56B VARIATION

Watch Your Skip!

SIGHTPLAYING HINT:
Be sure to **look** and **think ahead** at a tempo that will allow you to play smoothly!

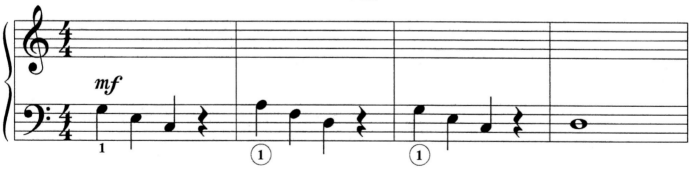

Lesson Fourteen total points ☐

Sightplaying Progress Report for Book 1

Accuracy:	Excellent	Good	Needs Improvement
Finds first note for each hand			
Plays correct rhythms			
Knows note locations on keyboard			
Knows note names on staff			
Recognizes intervals			
Uses good fingerings			
Notices dynamic marks			
Continuity (playing smooth and steady):			
Keeps eyes on music			
Looks and prepares ahead			
Keeps steady beat			
Keeps going after making a mistake			
Practice Habits:			
Follows sightplaying hints			
Counts one measure before starting			
Chooses good tempo (not too fast)			
Counts aloud while playing			
Uses metronome when assigned			

Teacher's Comments:

Congratulations to

_____

*for successfully completing **Let's Sightplay! Book 1***

Total earned points ☐
(Lessons One – Fourteen)

_____
Date

_____
Teacher